THE SMALLPOX

SLAYER

One Man's Fight Against
a Deadly Disease

Alan Brown

Hodder
Children's
Books

a division of Hodder Headline Limited

To the memory of James Phipps (1788-1853)

The author gives grateful thanks to the staff of
The Jenner Museum in Berkeley, particularly
Dr Malcolm Beeson, for all their help in the
writing of this book. Needless to say, they are not
responsible for any shortcomings it may have.

Text copyright 2001 © Alan Brown
Published by Hodder Children's Books 2001

Picture 1: Copyright © The Jenner Museum, Berkeley
Picture 2: Copyright © Parke Davis & Co. Limited. Image supplied by
The Jenner Museum, Berkeley
Picture 3: Copyright © The Jenner Museum, Berkeley
Picture 4: Image supplied by The Jenner Museum, Berkeley
Book design by Joy Mutter
Cover illustration by Stuart Haygarth

The right of Alan Brown to be identified as the author of the work has
been asserted by him in accordance with the Copyright, Designs and
Patents Act 1988.

10 9 8 7 6 5 4 3 2 1

A catalogue record for this book is available from the British Library.

ISBN: 0 340 78773 2

Printed by The Guernsey Press Company Limited.

Hodder Children's Books
a division of Hodder Headline Limited
338 Euston Road
London NW1 3BH

Contents

	Foreword	4
1.	James Phipps	6
2.	Smallpox	11
3.	Edward Jenner's Ordeal	16
4.	Jenner's Life	21
5.	The Royal Experiment	32
6.	What Happens to James?	36
7.	The Fight for Vaccination	44
8.	The Petition	50
9.	The Prize!	60
10.	Fame for Jenner	64
11.	A Life's Work	71
12.	An End to Smallpox!	81
	Time Line for Edward Jenner	90
	Glossary	91
	Further reading	94
	Index	96

Foreword

In HG Wells' fantastic book *The War of the Worlds* (1898) the invaders from Mars were "slain, after all man's devices had failed, by the humblest things that God, in his wisdom, has put upon this Earth."

These make-believe Martians had no resistance to germs which ". . . have taken their toll of humanity since the beginning of things."

The scientific name for germs is 'microbes'. What HG Wells said about them is true. We would not be healthy without them, but they can also make us sick. Some can kill.

The book you are now reading will take you on a journey to learn about the germs that cause disease. You will find out about one disease in particular, one doctor above all, and the child who helped to make a great discovery.

The fearsome disease is called 'smallpox'. In days past, it killed and maimed millions of people. The doctor is Edward Jenner. He lived many years ago, in England, before many people knew about germs. Microscopes were not very good, and few people had seen germs.

There are more microbes than any other living thing, but they are so small that hundreds of thousands would fit on to the dot of this letter 'i'! Today, our microscopes are much more powerful, and we can see microbes clearly. You have probably seen them on TV.

We take the existence of a microscopic living world for granted, but think what it was like when Jenner was alive. Look at the craters on the body of a smallpox victim in picture 4 in the middle of this book. Who would imagine that this is caused by something too small to even see?

Edward Jenner was a scientist as well as a doctor. He did not know about microbes, but he did experiments to find a way to stop people catching smallpox.

We will follow him like detectives, and his journey of discovery will be ours. At the end is a great reward – knowledge and health for the world.

At the start is a frightened boy of eight years old. His name is James Phipps. . .

James Phipps

A BOY OF EIGHT YEARS OLD is sitting in a country doctor's surgery. He is simply dressed, a poor labourer's son. His parents are waiting outside in the hall.

The boy's name is James Phipps, and James is afraid. He is afraid of what he knows is going to happen, and he is afraid of what he knows might happen. He bites his lip to stop himself from crying and the doctor says that he is a brave boy.

The doctor is smartly dressed in a long black coat with a large collar and tails. He wears a black waistcoat, loose-fitting trousers, white stockings and shiny black shoes. These are fashionable clothes for a gentleman in 1796. He is short in height, with dark, curly hair. He jokes with James, but the boy does not trust himself to reply.

The doctor rolls up James' sleeve. The boy's face and neck are brown from the sun, but his arm is pale. The doctor sorts through his instruments and chooses a sharp lancet.

James wants to run home. He could leave the grown-ups far behind, by crawling through hedgerows and running across the fields.

Then James thinks of his parents, waiting in the hall, and he squirms on his seat, but he does not run.

The doctor takes hold of James' arm and makes soothing noises, as if he is treating a nervous dog.

"What do you think of my new painting?" he might say, nodding at a picture on the wall.

When the boy looks up the doctor cuts his arm with the lancet, once, twice.

The cuts are small, but they sting and bleed. This is what James knew would happen. He had hurt himself worse than this just playing in the woods, but it was hard to sit still and let somebody else do it on purpose.

There are other people in the room. One is Sarah Nelmes, a dairymaid who has weeping sores on her hand. She has caught a disease called 'cowpox' from the cattle she milks every day. The word 'pox' describes these sores and the scars they leave.

The doctor scrapes at Sarah Nelmes' sores with the lancet. When he has some slimy gunge on the end, he smears it into the cuts on James Phipps' arm.

He is trying to make James sick with Sarah's illness! A doctor, deliberately giving somebody a disease!

Writers of this time used grand language – especially when they wanted to impress. Here are Jenner's own words:

"I selected a healthy Boy about eight years old for the purpose of inoculation for the Cowpox. The matter was taken from a suppurated sore on the hand of a Dairy Maid who was infected by her Master's Cows, and it was inserted on the 14th of May 1796, by means of two superficial incisions, each about three quarters of an inch long."

He binds up James' arm and sends him home.

A few days later, James has a temperature and the cuts on his arm turn into the same kind of sores that Sarah Nelmes had on her hand. But he is not very worried about this – he knows that nobody ever died from cowpox.

But two weeks later James is back in the doctor's surgery, and he is really frightened. Sarah Nelmes is not there. This time he is not going to be given a harmless disease like cowpox.

He can hardly sit still, and the doctor's wife has to hold him down. He wants to call out to his parents in the hall, but he knows that they will not help him.

Once again the doctor fetches out his lancet, and James is not fooled into looking away.

Whilst James peers at his bleeding arm, the doctor pokes at something in a little jar. He gets some of the stuff on a stick. It looks dirty and slimy, and the doctor keeps his nose well away.

The doctor's wife stoops with a rustle of starched petticoats. She holds James' arm, whilst the doctor pushes the slimy gunge into the gaping wound.

Then they bind the arm with bandages, careful not to get any of the slimy stuff on themselves.

They are careful for a good reason. This gunge is from somebody who is battling for life!

The doctor has given James a deadly disease that kills lots of people, covering their bodies with horrible sores. This disease is smallpox.

James is terrified about what will happen next.

Smallpox

WHY WOULD A DOCTOR deliberately infect anybody with a killer disease? Doctors swear to save lives, not to take them. The oath of the ancient Greek doctor, Hippocrates, says:

"I swear by Apollo the healer, invoking all the gods and goddesses to be my witnesses, that . . . the regimen [treatment] I adopt shall be for the benefit of the patients according to my ability and judgement, and not for their hurt or for any wrong. I will give no deadly drug to any. . ."

James Phipps was taking part in a medical experiment in 1796, over two hundred years ago. The doctor was Edward Jenner. At that time, smallpox was a disease that killed one in every four children.

If you had lived then, one of your brothers or sisters would probably have died of smallpox. It might have been two. It might have been you.

The disease was normally caught by breathing near somebody who already had the disease and who was coughing into the air. It could quickly spread through a whole family.

The first signs of smallpox are a bit like flu – high temperature, tiredness, headache and aching joints. After about a week, weeping sores erupt on the victim's skin, sometimes covering their entire face and body (see picture 4).

Sometimes there is bleeding inside the body, and black vomit. If the victim survives, the sores scab over, and when the scabs fall off a white scar or pock mark is left. Of all people who fell ill with smallpox, about one in five died.

Adults were less likely to catch smallpox than children. This was because most people did not catch smallpox twice. In the first illness, their bodies learned to resist the disease.

So, if you survived smallpox as a child, you wouldn't catch it again when you grew up. Also, if you did catch smallpox for the first time as an adult, you were stronger than a child, and more likely to survive.

But, as we've already discovered, even if you were not killed by smallpox, your skin was often badly scarred by pock marks. At that time, it was the fashion for both men and women to hide their faces under thick layers of powder and make-up.

Some survivors were blinded by smallpox. Many of these were children. So you can see why James Phipps was afraid.

Smallpox was a killer in ancient China, India and Egypt. It spread to Europe and was then carried round the world by explorers in the Middle Ages.

In the wars of conquest in the Americas, more of the native people were killed by smallpox than by the conquerors. None of the natives had caught it before, and so no one was resistant to the disease.

When Cortez of Spain invaded Mexico, three

and a half million Aztecs died of smallpox. When the English and other European nations invaded North America, six million Native Americans ('Indians') died of smallpox. The invaders sometimes spread the disease deliberately. It was safer for them than fighting.

Once smallpox was in a country, its people died from it all the time. This is different to a disease like the plague, that killed large numbers of people very quickly and disappeared again.

Smallpox was spread most easily when large numbers of people were gathered together, in armies, for example. In past times, victory in war has often followed an outbreak of smallpox amongst the enemy troops.

An invasion of England by France and Spain in 1779 was stopped by smallpox amongst the crew of the warships. When Prussia (a former German kingdom) defeated France in 1870, it was mostly because so many French soldiers were ill with smallpox.

Smallpox affects everybody who comes into contact with it, whoever they are. It has killed poor people and kings like Joseph I of Austria, Louis I of Spain, Peter II of Russia, Louis XV of France, Emperor Komei of Japan, and William of Orange and his wife Mary in England.

Famous people who have caught smallpox and survived include the rulers Elizabeth I and Louis XIV, the composer Mozart, and the American Presidents George Washington, Andrew Jackson and Abraham Lincoln.

Will James Phipps survive?

Edward Jenner's Ordeal

A BOY OF EIGHT YEARS old is kept hungry for weeks. He is made to drink foul potions to empty his stomach. Some of his blood is drained away. Then a cut is made in his arm and smallpox pus is poked into it.

He is bundled into a stable with other children who have all been infected with smallpox. The door is locked and they are left alone, to see who will live and who will die.

This is what happened to Edward Jenner when he was a child. It was called inoculation or 'variolation' – giving people smallpox on purpose so that those who survived would be safe from the disease.

If this seems cruel, remember how little was known about disease in those days. Few people believed that disease could be caused by creatures smaller than the eye can see. Microscopes were much less powerful than they are today.

In 1680, the Dutch scientist Antony Van Leeuwenhoek was one of the first people to find tiny living creatures under a microscope. He looked at scrapings from around his own teeth, and saw, "little animals more numerous than all the people in the Netherlands and moving about in the most delightful manner." He called them 'animalcules'.

In 1762, a Viennese doctor called Marcus Plenciz argued that infectious diseases, such as smallpox, were spread through the air by animalcules. He had no real evidence for this, and was not taken seriously.

Today, we call such tiny creatures 'microbes' – germs, in everyday speech. We know that many illnesses are caused by germs, and we call this 'infection'.

When Edward Jenner was a child, and even forty years later when James Phipps was the same age, most people thought that disease was caused by air that smelled bad, called 'miasma'. They thought perfume would make it safe!

Medical science had not improved much on the ideas of ancient Greece and Persia. Bleeding the patient, either through a vein or by applying blood-sucking leeches was thought to be a good idea.

We now know that bleeding and starvation are likely to make things worse by making the patient weak.

Inoculating children like Edward Jenner was not based on science. It was based on the common knowledge that people do not catch smallpox twice, without understanding why this was so.

The doctor looked for someone who seemed to have a mild case of smallpox, and infected other people from them. Everybody hoped that this would be less likely to kill than accidental infection later on.

In fact, the person doing the inoculations might

not be a doctor at all. Inoculation was first carried out in England in 1721 by Lady Mary Wortley Montagu. She brought the idea from Turkey, where her husband had been British Ambassador. It was introduced in America by Cotton Mather and Zabdiel Boylston that same year.

It did seem to work. On average, one person died in every two hundred who were inoculated. This is a lot better than the one in five who died from accidental infection.

But it was still a risky business. Sometimes, lots of people died. Sometimes, the people who had been deliberately inoculated infected others by accident. As time went by, it was gradually realised that inoculation with smallpox was actually spreading the disease.

We do not deliberately infect people with deadly live diseases any more. Getting protection against disease has been made safe. However, it was not safe when Edward Jenner was inoculated, hundreds of years ago. He might die, be blinded, or scarred for life.

Three weeks after Jenner was imprisoned in the barn, the door was thrown open and he staggered out, blinking like an owl in the sun. He was alive, but deeply affected in his mind. Others in the barn were not so lucky. The smell of death and decay must have been appalling. Years later, as a doctor, Jenner was determined to find a better way to fight the killer disease.

By a strange quirk of fate, his efforts led him to inflict a similar ordeal on the young James Phipps. Why did he do this?

Jenner's Life

E DWARD JENNER WAS BORN ON 17th May, 1749 in Berkeley, Gloucestershire, England. This was a country district of green fields with many dairy cattle. At that time, Berkeley had about two thousand people living in five hundred houses. It is also the site of Berkeley Castle.

When Edward was five years old, his mother and his clergyman father died. Edward was looked after by his eldest brother, Stephen, who was also a clergyman. The young Jenner must have been brought up with a strong sense of duty, and of right and wrong.

He said later of his research into smallpox, "I

shall myself continue to prosecute this inquiry, encouraged by the pleasing hope of its becoming essentially beneficial to mankind."

His great love of nature blossomed in the countryside. He learned to watch wild creatures closely and to write down exactly what he saw. In science, this is called 'observation'. It is one of the skills that Jenner needed later in the fight against smallpox.

He went to grammar school and then became the apprentice of a local surgeon. At thirteen, Edward started his medical training, learning how to do operations. People didn't spend so long at school in those days – they were expected to earn their keep!

When Jenner finished his apprenticeship at twenty-one, he still had a lot to learn. He went to London and worked with John Hunter, who was one of the most famous surgeons of his time.

He lived in London until he was twenty-four. John Hunter became his friend for life, and they sent each other many letters after Jenner moved back to Berkeley.

Hunter helped Jenner to get an important scientific job. This was to sort the specimens brought back by Joseph Banks from Captain Cook's first voyage of exploration to the South Seas.

Hunter also asked Jenner for help to find out how hedgehogs hibernate in winter. In a letter of 2nd August, 1775 he encouraged Jenner to experiment, as Jenner later did on James Phipps.

". . . why do you ask me a question by the way of solving it? I think your solution is just: but why think, why not try the experiment? Repeat all the experiments upon a hedgehog as soon as you receive this, and they will give you the solution."

Together, they discovered that it is the cooling of the hedgehog's body that causes it to hibernate.

Long before aeroplanes were invented, Edward Jenner became the first balloonist in England! He copied his balloon from the ones being developed in France, where the Montgolfier brothers were experimenting with balloons filled with hot air. Jenner's was so small that all it could carry was a poem of celebration! But he did make it himself, and hydrogen gas to fill it. It was a real scientific achievement when Jenner's balloon flew from Berkeley Castle in 1783.

The balloon was also important in another way. The second flight was made from a village in Gloucestershire called Kingscote. There Edward Jenner met Catherine Kingscote, who later became his wife.

Edward Jenner's next investigation was into the breeding of cuckoos. The cuckoo mother deposits its eggs in the nests of small birds, which rear the chicks as their own. The puzzle to be solved was how the original babies are thrown from the nest to make room for the young cuckoo to grow.

The nests to be studied were on a farm near Berkeley belonging to Jenner's aunt. His sixteen year-old nephew Henry was supposed to tour the nests each morning and report what he saw. From Henry's observations, Jenner wrote a paper saying that the foster parents threw out their own chicks.

However, Jenner must have had his doubts. The

tour of the nests involved a trek of six miles in total, and perhaps he knew that Henry was a bit lazy!

Jenner made more careful observations of his own and realised that the tiny baby cuckoo is the villain. It has a hollow between its wings that it uses to carry the other babies to the edge of the nest and tip them out.

For his research on cuckoos, Jenner was made a Fellow of the Royal Society. This was a great honour, because the Royal Society is a sort of club for famous scientists. Being invited to join must have given Jenner great confidence in his abilities.

On 8th March 1788, he married Catherine Kingscote, and on 24th January 1789 their first child was born. It was a boy and they called him Edward after his father.

Jenner was a popular doctor, and in those days doctors were paid by their patients for everything they did. Catherine also had money of her own, so Jenner's family was quite rich.

They lived in a fine old house called The Chantry. Jenner was very happy. He wrote to his friend Edward Gardner to say that the past year:

"has been the happiest beyond all comparison I have ever experienced. . . if you could be lucky enough to connect yourself with a woman of such a disposition as kind fortune has, at last, given me, you will find a vast addition to your stock of happiness."

However, Catherine's health was poor and the Jenners spent the summers at Cheltenham Spa. The water there is supposed to make you well, if you drank it, or bathed in it – but it did not make Catherine much better.

Edward treated patients in Cheltenham. Whilst he was there, in 1792, he was awarded a doctor's university degree (MD) by St. Andrews University, Scotland. Jenner never actually went to St. Andrews, but his friends swore that he had been to lectures and claimed he was worthy of the MD. As a result, the university sent his degree by post!

This was quite normal in those times. Edward Jenner needed a degree to be accepted everywhere as a doctor, but he had already been properly trained as an apprentice surgeon. Now his medical training was complete.

Jenner did research into other illnesses in these early years. He suggested that heart disease could be caused by the arteries becoming blocked. In 1778 he wrote:

"How much the heart must suffer from [the arteries] not being able to perform their functions is a subject I need not enlarge upon, therefore I shall only remark that it is possible that all the symptoms may arise from this one circumstance."

Jenner's good friend and teacher John Hunter himself died of heart disease in 1793. It was a great loss, but it was followed the next year by a happy event – the birth of the Jenners' second child. It was a girl, and they called her Catherine, after her mother.

Edward Jenner was a handsome man and something of a dandy – a man of style, smartness and fashion. He rode on horseback to visit his patients. A friend described him as he was in middle age:

"He was dressed in a blue coat and yellow

buttons, buckskins, well-polished jockey boots, with handsome silver spurs, and he carried a smart whip with a silver handle. His hair, after the fashion of the times, was done up in a club, and he wore a broad-brimmed hat."

His brother Stephen painted him in later life, and wrote at the bottom of the picture:

"Doctor Jenner was below the middle stature. His hair was dark and a little inclined to curl and it was observed at his death he was not the least grey. He was rather near sighted but never made use of glasses. His dress was black, a large collar and the coat and loose low trousers the dress of the day."

Edward Jenner was not a simple country doctor. He was one of the 'gentry' whose family owned land. He had rich patients in Berkeley, Gloucester and Cheltenham. He also wrote poetry and played both the flute and the violin. Here is one of his poems, *To a Fellow Sportsman who Upbraided the Author with Being a Bad Shot*:

'Why thus abuse me, mighty Sirs,
And jeer me with your taunting Slurs?

You're only joking – sure.
Each breast with Horror wd. be fill'd,
Heavens! to think that I had kill'd
Whose Province 'tis to cure.'

He collected fossils and investigated many things that were not medical. He was one of a group of Gloucestershire scientists who called themselves 'The Fleece Society', because they met at the Fleece Inn.

Then in 1796, shortly before the experiment on James Phipps, Edward Jenner was an expert witness in a murder trial.

His nephew Henry – the one who had made such bad observations of cuckoos – was now a doctor himself. Henry had treated a man named William Reed for stomach pains and a bleeding head. The man died. Henry had his suspicions, and as part of an experiment, he fed some of the man's vomit to a dog. The dog died.

Henry asked his uncle to find out what was in William Reed's stomach. Jenner found that it contained arsenic and mercury, both strong poisons. Reed's wife Mary was arrested, tried and found guilty of murder.

But on to Edward Jenner's most famous work. How did it all start?

Many of Doctor Jenner's patients in Berkeley worked with cows. The Vale of Berkeley is still famous for its dairy cattle. It is likely that Jenner would have heard strange stories about the disease cowpox. People caught it from the cattle, and afterwards they did not seem to catch smallpox.

This theory was rumoured amongst country folk, but nobody knew if it was true. Nobody had studied it, made observations, counted cases and reported findings. In other words, it had not been looked at scientifically, and hardly anybody believed it. Doctors still inoculated people with smallpox itself.

An experiment was needed to discover the facts. In an experiment, things are made to happen so that the results can be carefully studied. Things that muddle the experiment are prevented from happening. For example, people might be deliberately infected with a disease, but they have to be healthy to start with.

When scientists agree that an experiment has been done properly, they believe the results. They can repeat the experiment themselves to be quite sure. If the experiment showed that cowpox gave protection against smallpox, doctors would have good reason to use it.

Testing the effect of cowpox on resistance to smallpox was an attractive idea for Edward Jenner. The experiment suited his logical mind and desire to do good, and the ideas came from his own natural environment. He was also encouraged by his medical friends.

There had been a famous experiment before on smallpox – one which had nothing to do with cowpox. This is now known as the 'Royal Experiment'.

Chapter 5

The Royal Experiment

ARE ALL MEN AND WOMEN EQUAL? Today perhaps, but it was not thought so in Jenner's time.

In 1721, the royal family of England were wondering whether to inoculate their children with smallpox. The doctor would take the disease from somebody who was not seriously ill and pass it on to the royal children, in the hope that it would not harm them. Then they would not catch smallpox again.

Inoculation was quite new in England, and Caroline Princess of Wales wanted to be shown that it was safe. She did not want to risk her own

32

children until it had been tried out on some common people first. The 'Royal Experiment' was announced in the London newspapers:

"A Representation having been made to his Majesty, by some Physicians, that the Smallpox may be Communicated by insition or inoculating, as some express it, and that it has been practic'd safely and with Success, as might be experienc'd if some proper Objects to Practice on, were found out. 'Tis assured that two of the Condemn'd Prisoners, now in Newgate, have, upon this occasion, offer'd themselves to undergo the Experiment, upon receiving his Majesty's most gracious Pardon. . ."

In fact, six 'proper Objects to Practice on' were found. In those days, people were executed for some crimes, and these particular prisoners at Newgate Gaol had been condemned to be hanged. They were promised a pardon in return for being inoculated with smallpox. If they lived!

Remember that inoculation at that time meant deliberately infecting a person with the disease itself. Pus from a smallpox sore or powder from a dried scab would be inserted ('insition') into a cut.

The prisoners had nothing to lose and probably thought that they were on to a good thing. Especially when it turned out that the experiment was a success! They were ill, but they all lived and went free.

The power of the inoculations to stop later attacks of smallpox was tested in only one of the ex-prisoners. Elizabeth Harrison was persuaded to nurse smallpox victims, and she did not catch the disease herself.

Princess Caroline was a great worrier and not yet convinced. She asked for a much bigger experiment in which all the orphans of London would be inoculated. However, she did not get as many subjects as she wanted, as it was too much work for the doctors! In the end, they inoculated six orphans with smallpox. Again, all were ill, but none died.

These children could not refuse. The government could do what it liked with prisoners and orphans. The King's lawyers said that, "the Lives of the persons [the prisoners] being in the power of his Majesty, he may Grant a Pardon to them upon Such Lawful Condition as he shall think fit."

Today we have all sorts of rules about how medical experiments can be done, but in the eighteenth century people were more worried about the release of criminals.

Princess Caroline was finally convinced, though no doubt her heart was in her mouth when smallpox gunge was pushed into the cuts on her children's arms. The royal children survived and inoculation became the fashion amongst well-to-do people across the country.

Inoculation was never as popular with poorer people, not least because the Christian Church taught that disease was God's way of punishing the wicked. Many clergymen taught that avoiding smallpox was the work of the devil!

Chapter 6

What Happens to James?

Ｈ OW BRAVE JAMES PHIPPS MUST BE, to stand in the doctor's surgery and let Edward Jenner infect him with one disease after another. In 1796, for all anyone knows, he might be dead by morning, or be covered with the burning sores of smallpox!

Imagine his thoughts during the long days afterwards, waiting for something bad to happen. Do those little cuts on his arm itch? I think they would. Does he lift up the edge of the bandage and look anxiously at the scabs? I bet he does.

He is just eight years old, but he knows about smallpox. He knows how it kills. He knows the scars it leaves. He sees them on the face of his mother as she stops him scratching the sore that erupts after the first infection. Will there be more, with the second infection? Will they spread to his body and erupt on his face, the sores of smallpox?

James bites his lip and tries not to cry. His parents look at each other. James wants to be cuddled and told that everything will be all right, but his mother will not touch him. Will James live or die?

The days pass and become weeks, and still James is healthy. The doctors examine him, and announce that the smallpox has not made him ill at all. His parents hug him with joy! Edward Jenner was right. The first infection with cowpox protected James against the second one of killer smallpox!

James Phipps was the first person who we know for sure was vaccinated against smallpox. 'Vaccine' is a name Jenner invented for cowpox that means 'from the cow'. This was one of the most important moments in the history of medicine. Jenner's was the first of many vaccines that have since saved millions of lives.

Jenner wrote in high spirits to his friend Edward Gardner:

"A Boy of the name of Phipps was inoculated in the arm from a Pustule on the arm of a young Woman who was infected by her Master's Cows. . . I was astonished at the close resemblance of the Pustules in some of their stages to the variolous [smallpox] Pustules. But now listen to the most delightful part of my story. The Boy has since been inoculated for the smallpox which as I ventured to predict produced no effect. I shall now pursue my Experiments with redoubled ardour."

The cowpox came from a red-brown and white cow called Blossom. In later years, Jenner sent hairs from Blossom to his friends, as mementoes. Her hide and horns are now in museums.

Doctor Jenner did not understand exactly what had happened in his experiment. We know now that diseases are caused by germs and our bodies recognise ones we have fought before. This makes us better prepared to fight them again. That is how inoculation with smallpox protects us from catching it again, if we survive the first infection.

But cowpox and smallpox are different diseases, caused by different germs. So how did Blossom's cowpox prepare James Phipps' body to fight smallpox? The answer is that cowpox and smallpox are special. They are caused by germs that are very, very much alike. They perhaps started out the same, long ago. They are so much alike that when our bodies learn to recognise and fight the one, they learn to recognise and fight the other.

The experiment on James Phipps was in two parts. The first part was the vaccination with cowpox. The second part was the inoculation with smallpox, to test whether he had been given protection or not. The second was the really scary part, when the young boy put his trust in Edward Jenner. That was when he might have died or been maimed for life. That was how James Phipps quite rightly became famous.

You would think that Edward Jenner would

have been called a hero as soon as he announced his discovery to the world. Not a bit of it! When he showed his paper to scientists in the famous Royal Society, they said he needed more evidence. His friend Joseph Banks was President of the Society. He was now Sir Joseph, honoured because of the important specimens that Jenner had helped him to sort years before.

Banks said that Jenner, "ought not to risk his reputation by presenting to the learned body anything which appeared so much at variance with established knowledge."

Jenner was too stubborn to give up that easily, but for a while there was no cowpox at Berkeley that he could use, so there was nothing he could do about it.

A year passed. Edward's elder brother Stephen, who had been like a father to him, died. The Jenners' third child was born. It was a second son who was christened Robert, after Mrs Jenner's brother.

Then cowpox returned, and Jenner gathered more evidence. He infected five-year-old William

Summers with cowpox taken straight from a cow. He then vaccinated several other people arm-to-arm in a chain of infection, starting with William and without going back to the cow.

Next, Jenner tested some of these vaccinations by trying to infect his patients with smallpox. He should, of course, have tested them all. He vaccinated his own infant son, but it did not work. Robert did not properly catch cowpox and was later inoculated with smallpox.

Jenner published his findings himself in 1798, in the now famous paper with the long title, *An Inquiry into the Causes and Effects of the Variolae Vaccinae, a Disease Discovered in Some Western Counties of England, Particularly Gloucestershire, and Known by the Name of the Cow Pox.* 'Variolae vaccinae' means smallpox of the cow. What a mouthful! You can see why the paper is usually called the 'Inquiry'.

Because cowpox seemed sometimes to disappear, it was important that the vaccine could be passed from person to person. In the Inquiry, Doctor Jenner said:

"These experiments afforded me much satisfaction, they proved that the matter in passing from one human subject to another, through five generations, lost none of its original properties."

He argued that vaccination with cowpox gave good protection against smallpox, and was much safer than inoculation with smallpox alone. He said of James Phipps:

"The first boy whom I inoculated [vaccinated] with the matter of Cow-pox, slept in a bed while the experiment was going forward, with two children who never had gone through either that disease or the Small-pox, without infecting either of them."

Three in a bed was quite common in those days. The children of poor families sometimes took turns to go to bed! Diseases usually infected everybody in the family, even when started deliberately. This made inoculation with smallpox itself very dangerous.

Cowpox was different, Jenner said. "A single individual in a family. . . might receive it without the risk of infecting the rest, or of spreading a distemper [smallpox] that fills a country with terror."

He claimed that vaccination with cowpox was better in every way than inoculation with smallpox. It was harmless and yet gave complete resistance to the killer smallpox. He said that vaccination should be used instead of inoculation.

"As I have never known fatal effects from cowpox and as it clearly appears that the disease leaves the constitution in a state of perfect security from the infection of the smallpox, may we not infer that a mode of inoculation [that is, vaccination] may be introduced preferable to that at present adopted."

Jenner carried out more research and wrote more papers arguing for vaccination. Still few people believed him. He did not have many friends in London, where most important doctors worked. He was not yet famous. He was a Fellow of the Royal Society, but that was for work on cuckoos.

Jenner sent out samples of his cowpox vaccine. One or two well-known doctors in London tried it, and the tide began to turn.

Chapter 7

The Fight for Vaccination

MORE AND MORE DOCTORS read Jenner's 'Inquiry' and realised how useful his work might be in fighting smallpox. Some made new vaccine by taking cowpox from their own cows.

Jenner sent out more vaccine. When he wrote to Jean de Carro in Vienna on 27th November 1799, he described his methods. Note that he used the word 'virus' to mean some kind of poison, not a germ as we do today.

"I have enclos'd two portions of the Virus taken from different subjects; & with the view of excluding Oxygen as much as possible, I have plac'd it between two pieces of Glass. The quantity is larger than it appears, as so much evaporation takes place in drying. When you make use of it, moisten it either by taking up a very small portion of water on the point of your Lancet, or by breathing upon it."

By 1801 doctors were reading the 'Inquiry' in Germany, Italy, France, Holland and Spain. Soon, thousands of people were vaccinated in those countries, and in Turkey, the Middle East, Ceylon (Sri Lanka), India and the Americas.

Many people still argued against vaccination. Some said it was against God's will. Others pointed to the occasional failures and said that it did not work. A few claimed that the vaccine was really smallpox itself or some other disease entirely.

It is true that the smallpox virus could become mixed up with cowpox vaccine. This seems to have happened at the London Smallpox and Inoculation Hospital in 1799. The doctor there was William Woodville. He said that the vaccine Jenner sent him caused sores as bad as smallpox.

Jenner and Woodville argued about why this

had happened. In the end, Woodville admitted that some of his patients might really have caught smallpox, from the "atmosphere of the Hospital, which these patients were necessarily obliged to inspire during the progress of the Cow Pox infection."

It is more likely that Jenner was right when he said that the vaccine had become mixed with smallpox at the hospital. He told de Carro not to worry about it:

"However I presume this surprise will cease when you are informed that on the 5th day after the Cowpox Virus had been inserted into one arm, the variolous [smallpox] virus was inserted into the other, in those whose eruptions resembled those of smallpox; & thus, in my opinion, the two diseases became blended."

The London Smallpox and Inoculation Hospital had already sent samples of cowpox vaccine to Europe and North America, dried on threads. Some of the vaccine must have been good, and some contaminated with smallpox. There were disasters where patients died, and people blamed Jenner.

Jenner's enemies said that any failures proved that everything he said was wrong. The trouble was that he had announced in public that vaccination gave complete protection against smallpox for a lifetime. In the 'Inquiry' he declared that:

"What renders the cow-pox virus so extremely singular is that the person who has been thus affected is for ever after secure from the infection of the smallpox. . ."

Jenner was right in general about vaccination, but he was claiming too much. The body remembers its past infections, but now and again it needs to be reminded by another vaccination – what we call a 'booster-shot'.

Cowpox could be found in other European countries, but not in the rest of the world. Within a year of reading about Jenner's work, Luigi Sacco had used cowpox in Italy to vaccinate 8,000 people against smallpox. He sent his vaccine to countries of the East and in another two years, 90,000 people were vaccinated.

Most early vaccinations were arm-to-arm. In 1803 the cowpox vaccine was taken to South America by the physician of the King of Spain. To keep the virus alive during the long journey by sailing ship, he took a 'cargo' of children and passed the infection from one to another for three years!

"What a glorious Interprize!" exclaimed Jenner. On that expedition, 230,000 vaccinations were done. Even more importantly, the vaccine was spread so that others could use it.

In sharing cowpox from arm to arm there is a danger of passing on other diseases and we would not use this method nowadays. Doctors learned over the years that vaccine could be carried more easily when the liquid part was dried or diluted with glycerine (the stuff we use to make jellies!). This meant that each person could have their own vaccine, instead of sharing arm-to-arm.

Jenner was helped to develop ways of keeping and carrying cowpox vaccine. He thanked Doctor Marcet for:

". . . the glasses you sent me for the

Picture 1: Dr Edward Jenner, artist W Pearce

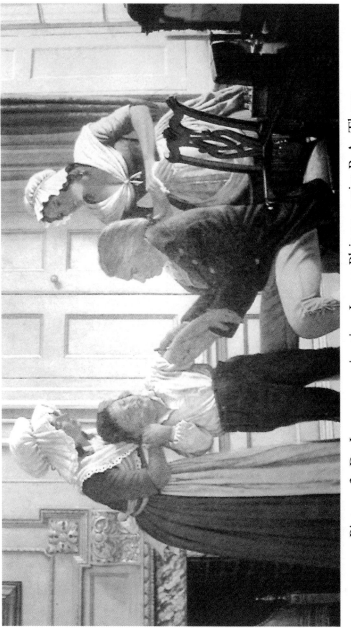

Picture 2: Dr Jenner vaccinating James Phipps, artist R.A. Thom

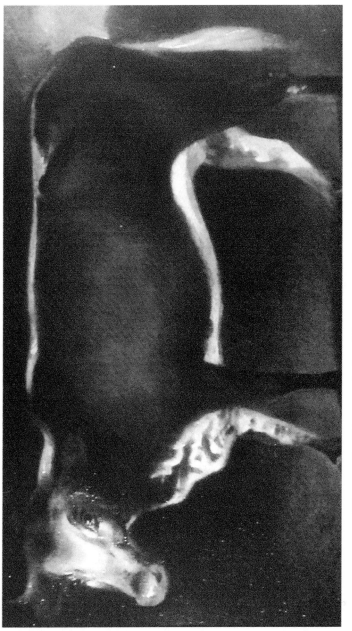

Picture 3: 'Blossom' the Gloucester Cow, artist unknown

Picture 4: Smallpox patient, Gloucester, 1923

preservation of Vaccine matter. . . At the expiration of three months, some Vaccine virus which I had accumulated on a quill, and suspended in a half-ounce phial, was used with complete success. . . from this virus the first patient ever inoculated in the metropolis received the Vaccine disease."

Considering that for most of the early 1800s there was war in Europe, and that there were no aeroplanes, only sailing ships, it is amazing how quickly vaccination spread to many parts of the world.

This tells us how people feared smallpox, and how desperate they were for a cure.

Chapter 8

The Petition

I F EDWARD JENNER HAD BEEN A greedy man he would have sold his vaccinations at a high price. He would have kept his methods secret so that others could not copy him.

In fact, he did everything he could to get the world to use cowpox vaccine against smallpox. He wrote many letters and published many papers talking about his discoveries. He sent the vaccine to other doctors so that they could use it too.

He carried on testing and experimenting so that he could answer every question about vaccination. If another doctor found that vaccination did not work, Jenner looked at their methods. He often found that they were not doing it right.

Vaccination became his personal crusade. "Every hour between Sun rising and Sun-setting brings me a Letter." He spent so much time encouraging vaccination that he earned less as a doctor than before. He complained in 1803 that people went to whoever would vaccinate them for the lowest price.

"Honours certainly fall in showers upon me, but Emoluments [money] fall off. You who possess a generous heart will feel indignant when I tell you that those identical People who last year brought their Children to me to be inoculated [vaccinated], now take their new born Little ones to their domestic Surgeon or Apothecary for that purpose – and why? They save perhaps a few Guineas by the exchange."

In 1802 Jenner asked the British Parliament to reward him for his work. This is called a petition. It was not so very unusual to be rewarded for public service. £20,000 was offered to anybody who could find a way to measure longitude at sea. That is the position of ships in an east-west direction. Many people competed for that prize.

At the time of Jenner's petition, £5,000 was given for a method of disinfecting warships, and it didn't even work! Not surprising when you remember how little was then known about germs.

Jenner had to struggle for his prize, in the same way that John Harrison struggled to win the longitude prize in the previous century.

George Pearson in particular objected to Jenner's claim, hoping to get the prize for himself.

Pearson worked in London with William Woodville of the London Smallpox and Inoculation Hospital. Both were friendly towards Jenner when he first published his work in the 'Inquiry'.

Then came the bitter dispute about the smallpox-like sores on Woodville's patients. It was Pearson who sent the contaminated vaccine round the world. Jenner later bitterly said, "He is one of those very extraordinary Beings who never committed an error." He meant that Pearson was so arrogant that he would never admit that he was wrong.

But by the time of the petition, Woodville and Pearson had vaccinated many more patients than Jenner, and they were better known in London.

Here are some of the arguments Jenner's enemies used against him. That he was not the first to use cowpox to protect from smallpox. A Dorset farmer named Benjamin Jesty was believed to have vaccinated his family twenty-five years before Jenner's experiments. That what Jenner had done was not so important compared to the work of other doctors, such as Woodville and Pearson! That vaccination with cowpox did not work. That the vaccine was not really cowpox, but a mild form of smallpox. If this was true, vaccination was no different to the old methods of inoculation.

Let us look at some of the answers.

Who vaccinated first? Jesty's claim was only made after Jenner wrote the 'Inquiry'. Would it ever have been made if the 'Inquiry' had not been published? Probably not. In any case, Jenner's work was the first that was at all scientific. He made careful observations of a number of patients, and published his findings so that other people could check them. It was his experiment on James Phipps that was the true start of vaccination.

Pearson did more vaccinations because he was grabbing every chance to make money. In 1799, a year after the 'Inquiry', he set up the Institution for the Inoculation of the Vaccine-Pock, to offer vaccination – at a price!

Jenner was busy doing research. He understood vaccination better than anyone. If things went wrong, people turned to him, not to Pearson.

There were two ways in which vaccine might be said not to work. It might cause an illness as serious as smallpox itself. Jenner's answer was that in this case the vaccine had become contaminated, and was smallpox itself. Doctors at this time did not know the importance of sterilisation. In a hospital where vaccination with cowpox and inoculation with smallpox were both done, it is easy to see how the two diseases could become mixed.

The other way vaccine might not work is by not protecting against smallpox as it was supposed to do. Jenner answered this by looking closely at where the vaccine had come from.

He found that some infections of cows looked a bit like cowpox but were not really cowpox at all. These gave no protection from smallpox, and he called them 'spurious' cowpox.

Jenner was ahead of his time in realising that there is some active part of the disease that gives protection. The vaccination has to cause a small illness in the patient (such as a pustule) or it has not worked.

Cowpox did not work if it was taken too soon or too late in its life in the cow. Jenner observed the stages of cowpox and described the best time to take vaccine.

When he was accused of using mild smallpox and calling it vaccine, Jenner described the sores that each made and showed that they were different. He could do no more with the knowledge of his time.

We could do better tests today, but the vaccine that Jenner used no longer exists. It has died out and new ones have been started.

It is interesting that modern vaccine is different

to both cowpox and smallpox, and seems not to have come from either. There is a possibility that Jenner was really working with horsepox, which also no longer exists. We shall never know!

The petition to Parliament showed that Jenner had many friends, as well as enemies. He was helped by his nephews Henry and George, old friends from school days such as Caleb Parry, and members of the Fleece Society such as John Hicks. All these were doctors who supported his claim.

He had impressed the whole Royal Family and most of the Government. Famous doctors and surgeons in London were now on his side. The Earl of Berkeley and the people of Gloucestershire gave a silver dinner service to Jenner, and petitioned Parliament on his behalf.

Official copies of Jenner's petition were lost in a fire many years later. He seems to have said to Parliament the same things that he wrote in *The Origin of the Vaccine Inoculation*, a paper published in 1801. In this he told how long and hard he studied cowpox. He said that, before his work, the idea that it could prevent smallpox was only vaguely and recently known. In this way he claimed the discovery as his own.

"My inquiry into the nature of the Cow Pox commenced upwards of twenty-five years ago. My attention to this singular disease was first excited by observing, that among those whom in the country I was frequently called upon to inoculate, many resisted every effort to give them the Small Pox. These patients I found had undergone a disease they called the Cow Pox, contracted by milking Cows affected with a peculiar eruption on their teats. On inquiry, it appeared that it had been known among the dairies time immemorial, and that a vague opinion prevailed that it was a preventative of the Small Pox. This opinion I found was, comparatively, new among them. . ."

Jenner admitted that some people caught smallpox after seeming to have already had cowpox. He argued that that was why doctors had not used vaccination before, and why his research was so difficult and important.

He said that mistakes had been made. Doctors

did not know about spurious cowpox and only thought their patients had cowpox. They did not understand the need to take true cowpox at the right time for it to work:

"This observation will fully explain the source of those errors which have been committed by many inoculators of the Cow Pox. Conceiving the whole process to be extremely simple, as not to admit of a mistake, they have been heedless about the state of the Vaccine Virus; and finding it limpid, as part of it will be, even in an advanced stage of the pustule, when the greater part of it has been converted into a scab, they have felt an improper confidence, and sometimes mistaken a spurious pustule, which the Vaccine fluid in this state is capable of exciting, for that which possesses the perfect character."

He described the experiment upon James Phipps and its happy result.

"This case [Phipps] inspired me with confidence; and as soon as I could again furnish myself with Virus from the Cow, I made an arrangement for a series of inoculations. A number of children were inoculated in succession, one from the other; and after several months had elapsed, they were exposed to the infection of the Small Pox; some by inoculation, others by various effluvia, and some in both ways; but they all resisted it. The result of these trials gradually led me into a wider field of experiment, which I went over not only with great attention, but with painful solicitude."

Jenner ended *Origin of the Vaccine* as he must have ended his petition, with a clarion call to defeat smallpox.

"A hundred thousand persons, upon the smallest computation, have been inoculated [vaccinated] in these realms. The numbers who have partaken of its benefits throughout Europe and other parts of the Globe are incalculable: and it now becomes too manifest to admit of controversy, that the annihilation of the Small Pox, the most dreadful scourge of the human species, must be the final result of this practise."

Edward Jenner had staked his claim to immortality.

The Prize!

A PARLIAMENTARY COMMITTEE WAS set up under Admiral Berkeley, brother of Jenner's friend the Earl. Jenner was asked to speak, but it seems he was too shy to do it!

"He himself. . . from singular diffidence, was incapable, even with preparation to give an oral testimony in public of what he thoroughly knew. He therefore delivered to the Committee a written statement."

Fortunately, others were less shy about speaking. King George III's own doctor, Sir Walter Farquhar, said, "I think it the greatest discovery that has been made for many years." Dr Matthew

Baillie of St George's Hospital called vaccination, ". . .the most important discovery that has ever been made in medicine."

Pearson seized upon Jenner's claim to have been the first person to use cowpox to prevent smallpox. He said that a number of people had done it before. These included Jesty the farmer, a farmer's wife named Rendell, a clergyman called Drew, a surgeon named Nash and a teacher named Platt.

It is likely that some of these were true, and it is a pity that Jenner made the claim he did. Jenner's contribution was really in the passing of the cowpox from person to person, so that vaccination could be done even when there were no infected cows. He used scientific experiment and observation to find out how to do this, and then he showed other people when he might have made a lot of money by keeping it to himself.

Had Jenner spoiled his chances? No, the petition was successful! Jenner was awarded a prize of £10,000!

It was not just the money that was important.

By giving Jenner this prize, Parliament was agreeing that vaccination was a good thing. In fact, they did not give Jenner the cash for another two years, and took £1,000 away in tax, so the prize did not solve all his money problems. To meet his living expenses and the cost of promoting vaccination, Jenner petitioned Parliament again, and in 1807 he was awarded another £20,000. Money was worth much more in those days. These prizes would be millions of pounds (US billions) today!

Jenner settled his dispute with William Woodville, which was about the methods of vaccination and not the value of vaccination itself. They agreed that cowpox can cause a rash beyond the vaccination site on the arm.

The row with George Pearson was personal and bitter. Jenner believed that Pearson wanted to take the credit for vaccination. "If Doctor P. could achieve his grand design of appearing as the efficient author of Vaccination, we should hear no more of its failures or imperfections."

Pearson was offended when Jenner refused to

be an "extra corresponding physician" in his (Pearson's) Institute for the Inoculation of the Vaccine-pock. Worse was to come.

Jenner spoke to Lord Egremont and the Duke of York, who were giving their names as supporters of the Institute. He persuaded them to take away their support. The Institute struggled on, but Pearson had become Jenner's lifelong enemy.

Fame for Jenner

JENNER WAS ACCEPTED AS THE father of vaccination. He met Queen Charlotte and the Prince of Wales. He rented a house in London and was called on by the Duke of York to vaccinate a regiment of soldiers. Vaccination was soon introduced in the British Navy.

The Royal Jennerian Society was set up in 1803, to give free vaccination to the poor. The Royal Family, William Wilberforce (who campaigned against slavery) and many other politicians supported the Society. In the early days, Jenner simply approved of the Society from his home in Berkeley. His fame in England was at its height.

George Pearson and others kept up a war of words in the medical journals, in newspapers, and by printing their own pamphlets (as Jenner had done). Dr William Rowley put up notices in London's public toilets denouncing vaccination!

One of the most active opponents of vaccination was Dr Benjamin Moseley, who Jenner called "that mad animal". In those days, authors often did not give their names, or they used a false one. A man called John Gale Jones campaigned against vaccination as Dr Squirrell!

Patients were found who had been properly vaccinated, but still caught smallpox. Jenner himself vaccinated people a second time if there was any doubt that the first had worked, but he would never admit that resistance to smallpox did not last a lifetime.

Jenner's opponents found out that he had inoculated his son Robert with smallpox itself. They said it showed that he did not think vaccination good enough for his own son.

It became a struggle to get poor people in

England's cities to accept even free vaccination. Many believed Jenner's enemies when they said that vaccination was dangerous. Others thought that it was not proper to use something that came from an animal. They believed that people were higher in the order of creation, and that vaccination would turn humans into brutes. Cartoons were printed in newspapers of patients growing horns!

In 1805, Jenner complained that the number of people being vaccinated in London was actually going down, and the number catching smallpox going up. Just when vaccination was becoming more and more popular abroad, it was becoming less popular at home.

Jenner wrote to Dr De Carro in Vienna, "In London my practice is limited to the higher orders of Society – In the Country, I can always find little Cottagers on whom I can introduce vaccine Virus in any form."

In 1807 The Royal College of Surgeons did a survey and found that out of 164,381 people vaccinated, 3 died, 56 later caught smallpox, and 90 had skin problems of some kind. This shows that vaccination was fairly safe, though not completely, and gave good protection against smallpox, though not complete protection.

Governments realised that vaccination saved them money, because of the better health of the people. Many countries made laws that said everybody had to be vaccinated, whether they wanted it or not. The Government in England was slow to do anything at all.

Jenner helped propose a law to ban inoculation with smallpox. He wrote impatiently that common sense should have been enough to make English people choose vaccination.

". . .how strange it is that such a Bill should be necessary. The records of Society, in modern times at least, afford no example of such a dereliction of common sense in any matter respecting self preservation, & in this particular matter before us, we the inhabitants of good old England stand alone, for it would be a libel to include our Neighbours the Scotch and Irish."

He saw that the struggles with the opponents of vaccination were wasting precious time.

"Take a survey of Europe and you will find that while we are fighting our Battles with the antivaccinists, they have been fighting with the Smallpox, & have vanquish'd the Monster."

Jenner's proposal to ban inoculation was turned down by Parliament. In England, inoculations with smallpox itself were made illegal in 1840, years after Jenner's death, and vaccination with cowpox was made compulsory in 1853.

A lot of people have always thought that compulsory vaccination robs them of their freedom. English law was changed to allow anyone the opportunity to refuse, so vaccination was not really compulsory any more.

In the United States, laws about vaccination were left for each state to decide. Jenner himself sent the first vaccine to America. One American doctor, named Benjamin Waterhouse, at first tried to make money by keeping vaccination to himself, but there was soon lots of vaccine sent from England.

Waterhouse then sent vaccine to the President of the USA, Thomas Jefferson. The President himself vaccinated his family and many Native

Americans in 1801. To keep vaccine cool, Jefferson made a special bottle that fitted inside a larger bottle filled with water. This made it easier to carry all over the country.

In Canada, Indians of the Five Nations were vaccinated after Chief Oughquagha John died of smallpox. The Governor made this speech to a gathering of the Mohawks, Onondagas, Senecas, Oneidas and Cayougas:

"So soon as your Brethren at the [River] Credit informed me that the Small Pox had appeared amongst them I hastened to their relief, attended by a skilful man in the service of Our Great White Father [the King] who by a safe and easy method of Inoculation [vaccination], lately found out on the other side of the Great Waters, will preserve by the assistance of the Great Spirit, the lives of many, who when we are no more, may become great Warriors and expert Huntsmen."

The Chiefs of the Five Nations sent Jenner a belt and string of Wampum-shell beads used by them as money. There were ten chiefs who thanked Jenner for saving their people. The names of the chiefs were Two Pointed Arrows, Two Wampum Belts, Clear Sky, Feather on His Head, Moving a Tree with Brush and Planting It, A Town Destroyer, Raven, Belt Carrier, A Disturber of Sleep, and Fish Carrier.

The father of vaccination was famous across the world.

A Life's Work

EDWARD JENNER DEVOTED THE rest of his life to promoting vaccination. For the first years of the 1800s he leased a house in London to be close to what was happening in the capital. He had so few patients in London that he lost £6000 in four years.

In 1803 he left London and never lived there again with his family. From Berkeley, and his other home in Cheltenham, he guided the course of vaccination in England, and wrote to vaccinators across the world.

James Phipps worked at The Chantry (the Jenners' house) as a handyman. He lived in Berkeley for the rest of his days. Jenner spent time on the Royal

Jennerian Society, quarrelling with John Walker, its chief vaccinator. Jenner was born into the English gentry – Walker was not at all genteel.

Despite their differences, Jenner supported Walker at first. But Walker's manner soon became a problem. He was arrogant with the free patients whom it was his job to vaccinate.

"The few mothers that had the courage to bring back their children for examination were frightened... Someone perhaps attempted to fly; Dr Walker leaped to the door, and barricaded it with his body, saying, "Thou foolish woman, if thou wilt not do good to others, I will bless thy little one," and forthwith drew his lancet. . . The screams of the terrified child, the complaints of the excited mother. . . did not intimidate the courageous soul of the director."

These free patients were the poor of London. According to the rules of the Royal Jennerian Society, they had to be sent by somebody in the Society – they could not just turn up. They were asked to come back several times to be examined, and all this during the day, when they might be working. It is not surprising that the poor were choosing not to be vaccinated!

Even Jenner saw the poor as inferiors. He is reported as saying about the poor of his parish, "You pass by these little Children as weeds. I treat them at least as vegetables."

Jenner was most offended when Walker argued about the proper way to vaccinate. This was something about which Jenner thought himself to be the number one expert. Walker's behaviour had become impossible to accept. After a long struggle, Jenner forced Walker out of the Royal Jennerian Society by threatening to leave himself if Walker remained. The Society never really recovered from this quarrel, and was soon disbanded.

Jenner persuaded the government to give money to a new organisation called the National Vaccine Establishment. John Walker had already set up the London Vaccine Institution, and the two competed for patients and recognition.

Walker often attacked Jenner in a journal called the Medical Observer. He even published a 'Jenneric Opera', that starts:

'There was a jolly Potiker [doctor] liv'd near

the Severn side,
    He mounted on a good fat cow, and a begging
he did ride.'

People were very rude to each other in those
days! William Howard, whose wife had died of
smallpox after being vaccinated, wrote a poem
attacking Jenner:

Weep Jenner weep and hide your head
Or blush in crimson like the Sun
Visit the mansions of the dead
And see the mischiefs you have done

Then view the falling pearly tear
That gushes from each orphan's eye
Ask them the cause and soon you'd hear
Jenner and Cow Pox they'd reply

Jenner was not very good at this public war of
insults. Perhaps it was not just shyness that
stopped him speaking in support of his own
petition to Parliament. Perhaps it was something

deeper. He much preferred writing to speaking, but even so he did not make such good use of the newspapers as his enemies did.

At some time in his life, Jenner joined the secret society of Freemasons. He was always a believer in God and a natural order: "The whole creation is the work of God's hands. It cannot manage itself. Man cannot manage it, therefore, God is the manager."

When Parliament gave Jenner the second prize in 1807, it was because it had been sent such glowing reports about vaccination. "The College of Physicians. . . feel themselves authorized to state that a body of evidence so large, so temperate, and so consistent, was perhaps never before collected upon any medical question. . ."

Even so, Jenner was often unhappy about the slow progress of vaccination in England, and what he saw as a lack of recognition for himself. He said that a reward of £4,000 from Calcutta in India had stopped him giving up completely:

"These marks of attention, my dear Friend, are very soothing to my feelings. Without them, I should very shortly have put into execution a resolution I had form'd which many of my Friends would, doubtless have thought desparate. It was nothing short of retirement from what is called the world. Not that partial exclusion, which admits of occasional visits & correspondence, but a total secession. . . However I begin to revive again. . ."

In fact, Jenner received many honours; money from other Indian states, gold medals, degrees from universities. He was granted the freedom of London and many other cities. This ceremonial handing over of keys giving the ancient right to come and go showed how highly people valued him.

He even used his influence to free medical men and relatives of friends who were held as prisoners by the warring nations of England, France and Spain. Napoleon Bonaparte was so grateful for smallpox vaccine that he said, "I can refuse Jenner nothing."

Jenner never agreed any fault with vaccination, and he would not work with anybody he suspected of disloyalty. Perhaps he made the fight against smallpox more difficult by trying to run it all himself.

In 1809 Jenner wrote, "The affairs of the National Vaccine Establishment go on badly. . .

The Board appointed me Director of course but they have contriv'd to let me know that I am the Director directed, for out of the eight names I nominated to fill the Vaccinating Stations, they have taken only two; the others are fill'd by men who are utter strangers to me, and what is still worse (indeed is it not insulting?) one of them who is appointed the Vaccine chief, & to superintend the other stations is sadly taken from Pearson's Institution to which he was Surgeon."

Asked to work with a henchman of his old enemy, George Pearson! Jenner soon left the National Vaccine Establishment, and lost most of his power in London. He was glad to no longer have to visit the capital.

After helping other people so much, tragedy struck Jenner's family. His eldest son, Edward junior, died of tuberculosis in 1809. "I had no conception till it happened that the gash would have been so deep; but God's will be done!" Jenner's wife Catherine also died of her tuberculosis at Cheltenham in 1815.

The world famous man retired to Berkeley,

where he became a magistrate (like a judge) and then Mayor. He completed work started many years before, showing that seasonal birds such as swallows flew away to other countries (migrated) in the autumn when the weather became cold. Before Jenner's accurate observations, many people thought that they hibernated in caves, like bats, or even below the ice in ponds, like fish!

In his last years, he was once again a busy country doctor. However, his own health was not good. He caught the usual illnesses of the age, such as cholera, and he always seemed to have felt what we call stress. He said in a letter:

"My dear Sir, I ought to make a thousand apologies to you for suffering your last obliging Letter to remain so long unanswer'd. Did my Friends whom I serve in this manner, but know the worrying kind of life I lead, they would soon seal my pardon."

Jenner gave free vaccinations to the poor of Berkeley in the 'Temple of Vaccinia', a strange grotto in the garden of The Chantry. The doctor was helped by Francis Hands, who said, "I. . . went to his House several times a day Sundays not excepted to assist in Vaccinating the poor who came from the surrounding neighbourhood of Five and Eight miles. It was my province to examine each candidate. . . to see that each person was in good health. Also to see that every person who was to be Vaccinated should be perfectly free from Worms of every sort. . ."

Edward Jenner, the pioneer of vaccination had a 'seizure' in the summer of 1820. This was probably a stroke, an illness where blood does not get through to the brain. He was discovered unconscious in the garden of The Chantry and put to bed.

The next day he seemed better, except for a limp. This kind of problem with arms or legs often happens after strokes. He was treated by having leeches suck his blood.

"I am getting better, in some measure from the lameness I mentioned to you, but I feel assured that I am not sufficiently sound to bear the motion of a carriage without a great risk."

Jenner complained that he could no longer bear sharp noises: ". . .the sharp clinking of Teacups and Saucers, Teaspoons, Knives & Forks on earthen Plates, so distract me that I cannot go into Society which has not been disciplined & learnt how to administer to my state of distress."

He tired easily: ". . . though I boast of my strength in a morning, yet evening seems to come before its time. My afternoon is all evening, and my evening midnight."

All Jenner's brothers and sisters were dead. He was an old man and the last in the family of his generation. One day he was found again unconscious, lying on the floor of the library. James Phipps was sent for help. Jenner was given the usual treatment of bleeding, but died the next day, 26th January, 1823. He was aged 73.

Edward Jenner was buried in the family plot in the Berkeley graveyard. No one came from London, but James Phipps was amongst the mourners standing in the winter snow. In his will, Jenner left James a house near The Chantry – rent-free for the rest of his life.

Jenner's goal of utterly defeating the 'horrid Monster Smallpox' was not achieved in his lifetime. But it was achieved, as we shall see.

An End to Smallpox!

EDWARD JENNER HIMSELF, right back when he was still struggling to get vaccination accepted at all, said that smallpox could be got rid of entirely from the face of the earth.

"The joy I felt at the prospect before me of being the instrument destined to take away from the world one of its greatest calamities. . . was often so excessive that. . . I have sometimes found myself in a kind of reverie."

It quickly became clear that mass vaccination would eradicate smallpox in small areas, and even whole countries – but only in rich places, with good medical treatment. For example, soon after getting vaccine from Jenner, the countries of Denmark and Sweden were able to get rid of smallpox almost entirely. Later, it fell to very low levels in the USA.

But even where the disease seemed a thing of the past, fresh epidemics suddenly returned. This happened in Jenner's county town of Gloucester in 1896 – one hundred years after the first vaccination!

The problem was that people coming into smallpox-free places could bring the disease with them. As late as 1961, there were 26 deaths in England from smallpox coming from Africa. For this reason, Canada set up quarantine stations for immigrants. People were only let into the country after they had been vaccinated and had no signs of smallpox.

So long as the disease existed somewhere, it could be carried across the world. This meant that everybody still needed to be vaccinated, even if there was no smallpox where they lived.

The rich countries finally realised that helping the poor countries get rid of smallpox would make life safer for everybody.

Large amounts of vaccine were needed and arm-to-arm methods were not good enough. Happily, in the latter part of the 1800s, it had become the custom to grow vaccine in calves. This way, large amounts of pure vaccine could be produced quickly.

Calves were kept for a while in an enclosed area which was a combination of a farm, factory and a laboratory. This was so that their health could be checked, and they were also washed and had their middles shaved. This part of their bodies was then vaccinated many times. Each vaccination site grew a sore from which more vaccine could be taken.

At first there was opposition to this 'animal vaccine'. However, it became popular because the vaccine worked so well, and did not pass on any other diseases.

But taking live animals from place to place was not always easy. Doctors found that adding glycerine (a kind of jelly) to the vaccine killed unwanted germs and made it easy to carry in a tube.

There were also improvements in the way the punctures in the patient's skin were made. It was always difficult to keep lancets free of unwanted germs. Eventually, a needle was invented that could be easily sterilised and which also used much less vaccine.

Taking vaccine to the hot tropics and keeping it in good condition was a problem not solved until the 1950s, when freeze-drying was invented. A long-keeping vaccine was then made in the same way as instant coffee!

Just as important as these difficulties was the problem of cooperation. To stand a chance of eradicating smallpox, every country in the world would have to work together.

It was the World Health Organisation (WHO) that finally brought everybody together. Then the stage was set for the final battle of Jenner's dreams!

The WHO Smallpox Eradication Campaign was launched in 1967. Russia gave 650 million doses of free vaccine, and the first step was to vaccinate as many people as possible in the shortest possible time.

Speed was necessary because people move

about. If vaccination had been done slowly, lots of people would have been missed when they moved to places where vaccination had already been done.

The next step was to search out any remaining smallpox victims. They were vaccinated and kept for a while in special 'isolation hospitals' where they could not spread the disease. Their friends and relatives were kept there too.

To persuade people to help the campaign, money was paid as a reward for finding victims of smallpox. Some people deliberately tried to keep the disease alive because they still believed that inoculation with smallpox itself was better than vaccination. The old argument, so long after Jenner had shown that it was wrong! Illegal stores of smallpox virus had to be destroyed.

Each country was declared free of the disease when no new cases of smallpox had been found there for two years.

Smallpox in India was the biggest problem. A huge number of people lived in little villages, so it was hard to get to everybody. In 1953 there were

253,332 cases of smallpox – more than the rest of the world put together!

After enormous efforts by thousands of medical workers, the WHO declared that India was free of smallpox in 1977.

The last person to catch smallpox in everyday life was a hospital cook called Ali Maow Maalin living in Somalia, Africa in 1977. He survived. Two years later, on 9th December 1979, the WHO declared that smallpox had been eradicated from the whole world.

"We, the members of the global commission for the certification of smallpox eradication, certify that smallpox has been eradicated from the world."

In the celebrations, Ali was presented with a bouquet of roses. The campaign cost 312 million dollars, but from this time vaccination could stop. Smallpox virus only exists now deep-frozen in two laboratories, one in the USA and the other in Russia. Let's hope it stays there!

To rid the world of a disease is a tremendous achievement. Can it be done with other diseases that cause misery and death? The answer is, perhaps.

To eradicate a disease, it has to be easy to identify and infectious for only a short time in each victim. Animals must not suffer from it, or people would keep catching it from them.

Of course, there also has to be a vaccine, or a treatment for the disease that is cheap and works well.

This was all true for smallpox. What about other diseases?

Polio is a good possibility. This is a crippling disease that ruins the lives of many children. The WHO is right now battling against polio across the world.

Tuberculosis (TB) – the disease that killed Catherine Jenner and Edward Jenner junior – was once thought to be a possibility. However, there are problems because it takes years to develop and is hard to cure, even with modern drugs. Even so, vaccination and good living conditions brought TB to low levels in the richer countries of the world.

Now tuberculosis seems to be increasing again. Many people have not bothered with vaccination, and are catching new forms of the disease that are coming from Eastern Europe. These new forms are even harder to cure than the old.

This takes us back to where we started. In the story *The War of the Worlds* we are saved by microbes that are harmless to us, but deadly to the Martians. HG Wells said, "These germs of disease have taken their toll of humanity since the beginning of things – taken toll of our prehuman ancestors since life began here. But by virtue of this natural selection of our kind we have developed resisting power. . ."

Natural selection is what happens over many years when children are born with something useful, like resistance to a disease, that they get from their parents.

The trouble is that natural selection works fast in microbes. They breed quickly and mutate, or change their forms. Our drugs kill off the weak, leaving the strong. So microbes develop resistance to medicine. This is how the new forms of TB have come about. Modern medicine has created superbugs!

It begins to look as if we can never completely

conquer nature. The world is a germy place and always will be. We must find ways to work with nature, as Jenner did. He gave us a natural vaccine. Without it, the World Health Organisation could not have defeated smallpox.

Smallpox is still the only disease that has been totally eradicated. For this wonder we must thank the WHO and the governments of nations. But our first and last thanks must be to Edward Jenner and, of course, to James Phipps.

Time Line for Edward Jenner

1749 Jenner's birth
1754 Death of parents
1761 Apprentice surgeon
1770 Studies with John Hunter in London
1785 Buys 'The Chantry' in Berkeley
1786 Studies cuckoos
1788 Marries Catherine Kingscote
1789 Elected Fellow of the Royal Society, birth of Edward junior
1792 Granted degree in medicine by St Andrews University
1793 Birth of second child, Catherine junior
1796 Vaccination of James Phipps
1797 Birth of third child, Robert
1798 Phipps experiment published, first vaccination in London
1799 First vaccination in USA
1802 First award by Parliament of £10,000
1803 Creation of Royal Jennerian Society
1806 Second award by Parliament of £20,000
1810 Death of son, Edward junior
1811 Vaccination made compulsory in Norway
1812 Granted honorary degree in medicine by Oxford University
1815 Death of wife, Catherine
1820 Jenner suffers first stroke
1823 Jenner's death

Glossary

Animal: in modern science, almost all living things that are not plants are animals. This includes human beings. But in Jenner's time, people thought that humans were a special and higher form of life.

Apothecary: a chemist who sells medicines from a shop.

Apprentice (Apprenticeship): a young person who learns a skill from somebody who already has that skill. An apprenticeship is a legal agreement between the two.

Booster shot: a repeat vaccination to increase resistance to a disease.

Contaminate: to get where it is not wanted. Particularly contamination by germs.

Cowpox: one of a number of pox diseases, this a mild one found now and again in cows.

Develop: to change or grow.

Disease: an illness caused by microbes.

Doctor: a person who has a high university degree, used here to mean a doctor of medicine who has a medical degree.

Eradicate: to get rid of something for ever.

Evidence: facts that show if an argument is true or false.

Experiment: to test an argument by changing some things whilst keeping other things the same.

Generation: a step in the lives of living things, in people from parents to children.

Germs: the smallest of living things, microbes.

Hibernate: to spend the winter with the body slowed like a deep sleep.

Incision: a small cut.

Infection: what happens when microbes get into the body.

Inoculate (Inoculation): to infect a person with a disease on purpose. In Jenner's time to infect with live smallpox (as in variolate). In modern times to infect with a disease which has been made harmless so as to give resistance to that disease.

Laboratory: a place where scientific experiments are done.

Lancet: a pointed knife used by doctors.

Microbes: the smallest of living things, commonly called germs.

Mutate: to change form.

Natural selection: the way living things that fit their surroundings best survive and pass on their characteristics.

Observation: to use senses such as sight to find out what is happening.

Paper: used here to mean a piece of writing about a subject.

Petition: to ask for something in writing, often with many people signing it.

Physician: another word for doctor of medicine.

Pock: a sore on the skin or the scar left by a sore.

Publish: to tell other people something, used here to mean putting it in writing and making lots of copies to give away or sell.

Pustule: a sore on the skin.

Quarantine: to keep somebody away from other people so that they do not pass on disease.

Quill: a sharpened feather, often from a goose. Quills were dipped in ink and used as pens.

Report: to tell about something. A paper telling and informing about something.

Research: to try to find out about something in a careful way that other people can repeat.

Resistance: to fight successfully against something such as a disease.

Science: the knowledge gained by using research and experiment.

Smallpox: one of a number of pox diseases, this one a killer of humans.

Specimen: an example of something from nature.

Spurious: not the real thing.

Sterilise: to kill all germs on or in something.

Surgeon (Surgical): a person trained to cure illness by carrying out operations on the patient's body, sometimes using cutting.

Survey: to find out what is happening by observing and counting.

Tuberculosis (TB): a serious disease affecting the lungs, once known as the 'White Plague'.

University: a place where people study for degrees.

Vaccinate (Vaccine): in Jenner's time to infect a person with cowpox on purpose, in modern times to infect with any disease that is no longer live, with the aim of giving resistance to that disease.

Variolate (Variolation): to infect a person with live smallpox on purpose, with the aim of giving resistance to that disease.

Virus: in Jenner's time some kind of poison, now a kind of microbe.

Further reading

Peter Baldry, *The Battle Against Bacteria: A Fresh Look,* Cambridge University Press, 1976.

John Baron, *The Life of Edward Jenner,* London: Henry Colburn, 1827.

Derrick Baxby, *Jenner's Smallpox Vaccine: The Riddle of Vaccinia Virus and Its Origins,* London: Heinemann, 1981.

Derrick Baxby, *Vaccination: Jenner's Legacy,* Berkeley: The Jenner Educational Trust, 1994.

Herve Bazin, *The Eradication of Smallpox,* San Diego: Academic Press, 2000.

William R Clark, *At War Within: The Double-Edged Sword of Immunity,* Oxford University Press, 1995.

F Dawtrey Drewitt, *The Life of Edward Jenner,* Longmans, 1931.

Richard B Fisher, *Edward Jenner,* London: Andre Deutsch, 1991.

Canon J E Gethyn-Jones, *The Chantry,* Berkeley: Jenner Museum.

Fenner F, Henderson D, Arita I, Jezek Z, Lodny ID, *Smallpox and Its Eradication,* Geneva: WHO, 1988.

Edward Jenner, *Inquiry into the Causes and Effects of the Variolae Vaccinae,* London: Sampson Low, 1798.

Edward Jenner, *Further Observations on the Variolae Vaccinae, or Cow Pox,* London: Sampson Low, 1799, 1800.

Edward Jenner, *A Continuation of Facts and Observations Relative to the Variolae Vaccinae, or Cow Pox,* London:

Sampson Low, 1800.

Edward Jenner, *The Origin of the Vaccine Inoculation*, London: D N Shury, 1801.

W R LeFanu, *A Bio-Bibliography of Edward Jenner*, London: Harvey and Blythe, 1951.

Genevieve Miller, *Letters of Edward Jenner*, Baltimore: John Hopkins University Press, 1983.

Peter Razzel, *Edward Jenner's Cowpox Vaccine: The History of a Medical Myth*, Firle, Sussex: Caliban Books, 1977.

H G Wells, *The War of the Worlds*, Everyman, 1993.

The Jenner Museum is situated in Edward Jenner's beautiful house The Chantry, in Berkeley, Gloucestershire. The Museum has informative displays and the 'Temple of Vaccinia' can still be found in the lovely garden. Jenner literature is supplied by post from: The Jenner Museum, Berkeley, Gloucestershire, GL13 9BH, UK.

Index

arm-to-arm method 41, 48, 83

Berkeley 21, 24, 28, 30, 40, 64, 71, 77, 78, 80

Blossom 38, 39

Chantry, The 25, 71, 78, 79, 80

Cheltenham 26, 28, 71, 77

cowpox 8, 9, 30-1, 37, 39, 40-1, 42-3, 44, 46, 47, 53, 55, 56, 57, 58, 61
    spurious cowpox 55, 58
    vaccination 37, 41, 42, 43, 47, 48, 53, 54, 61, 62-4, 66, 67, 68, 73, 76, 78, 81
    vaccine 43, 45, 46, 48, 50, 54, 55, 83

Fleece Society, The 29, 56

germs 4, 5, 17, 38, 83, 88-9

Inquiry, the 41, 44, 45, 47, 52, 53, 54

Jenner, Catherine (child) 27
Jenner, Catherine (wife) 25, 77
Jenner, Edward 4, 6-7, 21-31
    childhood 16, 17, 19-20, 21, 22
    cuckoo investigation 24-5
    death 80
    fame 64-70, 76
    ill health 78-80
    medical training 22, 23, 26-7
    migration investigation 78
    rewards 61, 62, 75-6
    smallpox research 21-2, 43, 54
    vaccination crusade 43, 50-9, 60-3, 65-6, 71-81
Jenner, Edward (child) 25, 77
Jenner, Robert (child) 40, 41, 65
Jenner, Stephen (brother) 21, 28, 40

Kingscote, Catherine 24

London Smallpox and Inoculation Hospital 45, 46, 52
London Vaccine Institution 73

microbes 4, 5, 17
microscopes 5, 17
modern vaccine 55-6, 84-8

National Vaccine Establishment 73, 76-7
natural selection 88
Nelmes, Sarah 8, 9

opposition 40, 43, 45, 46-7, 52-9, 61-3, 65-6, 67-8, 73-4, 83, 85

Petition, the 50-9, 60-1, 62, 75
Phipps, James 5, 13, 15, 42, 58, 71, 80, 89
    experiment 6-10, 11, 29, 36-9, 42, 58

Royal College of Surgeons 66
Royal Experiment 31, 32-5
Royal Jennerian Society 64, 72-3
Royal Society 25, 40, 43

smallpox
    eradication 84-9
    inoculation 16, 18, 19, 30, 32-5, 39, 42, 43, 54, 57-9, 67, 68
    resistance 12-3, 18, 30-1, 57, 65
    symptoms 12
sterilisation 54, 84
Summers, William 40-1

Temple of Vaccinia 78-9
tuberculosis 77, 87, 88

World Health Organisation 84-7, 89
worldwide cases 13-4, 82, 85-6
worldwide vaccination 45, 46, 47-8, 49, 59, 67-70, 75, 82, 84-6